A BOOK OF POSTCARDS

NEW YORK CITY

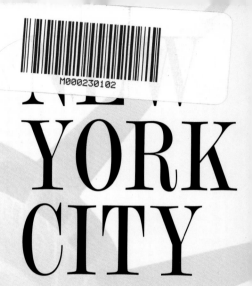

Pomegranate

SAN FRANCISCO

Photographs from
The New York Times
Expect the World®

Pomegranate Communications, Inc.
Box 808022, Petaluma, California 94975
800-227-1428
www.pomegranate.com

Pomegranate Europe Ltd.
Unit 1, Heathcote Business Centre, Hurlbutt Road
Warwick, Warwickshire CV34 6TD, U.K.
(44) 01926 430111

ISBN 0-7649-2551-2
Pomegranate Catalog No. AA221

Pomegranate publishes books of
postcards on a wide range of subjects.
Please contact the publisher for more information.

Cover designed by Gina Bostian
Printed in China

12 11 10 09 08 07 06 05 04 03   10 9 8 7 6 5 4 3 2 1

To facilitate detachment of the postcards from this book, fold each card along its perforation line before tearing.

Photojournalism confronts an unfolding drama and freezes the frame, refusing to let the fleeting instant flee. It stops the world at that moment of history and lets us get on.

—William Safire, *The New York Times*

The first photographic halftones appeared in *The New York Times* in the inaugural issue of its *Illustrated Sunday Magazine* in 1896—sixteen years after the *New York Daily Graphic* became the first newspaper to publish a photographic halftone, and forty-five years after *The Times* was founded.

It was not until 1910 that *The Times* published a photograph on the front page, of aviator Glen Curtiss taking off from Albany on the first nonstop flight to New York City. *The Times* extravagantly hired a train, stocked with reporters and a photographer, to track the flight. Over the years, *The Times* made several forays into competitive photojournalism, scooping stories by securing exclusive access for its photographers, or altogether sponsoring great discoveries. *The Times* bankrolled Admiral Byrd's 1928–1931 Antarctic expedition and nabbed exclusive rights to cover Charles Lindburgh's famed 1927 transatlantic solo flight and Howard Carter's 1922 opening of the 3,300-year-old tomb of King Tut-Ankh-Amen in Luxor, Egypt.

With the extensive photography of the First World War, *New York Times* publisher Adolph Ochs started the *Mid-Week Pictorial War Extra*. Here, *The Times* took the lead in defining modern photojournalism. The name changed in 1915 to the *Mid-Week Pictorial* as its focus broadened beyond the war, and it remained a separately sold publication until 1936, the year *Life* magazine was launched.

During the run of the *Mid-Week Pictorial*, *The Times* leveraged its newfound strength in news photography and began its Times World Wide Photos syndicate, which it sold in 1941 to the Associated Press. Times World Wide gathered and distributed news photographs globally, further enhancing the reach of *The New York Times* and its photographers. Throughout the 1920s, *The Times* built up its team of staff photographers, and for a generation it (and all newspapers) enjoyed the role of being the source through which most people first encountered images of the news.

Since the advent of broadcast news, the aesthetic of photojournalism has changed, but the value of the still photograph to the reader and to the news has not diminished. The still photograph may no longer be the only image—or even the first image—one sees, but photojournalism tends to capture the image we remember, the iconic symbol of an era or event.

While the reach of *The Times* has always gone far beyond New York City, this selection of images is a tribute to *The Times*'s hometown, perhaps the most photographed city in the world.

Source (and for further reading): Peter Galassi and Susan Kismaric, *Pictures of the Times: A Century of Photography from The New York Times* (The Museum of Modern Art, 1996).

NEW YORK CITY
Photographs from **The New York Times**

Times Square, 1919
The New York Times Photo Archives

BOX 808022   PETALUMA   CA 94975

Pomegranate

NEW YORK CITY
Photographs from **The New York Times**

Sherry-Netherland Hotel fire, 1927
The New York Times Photo Archives

BOX 808022   PETALUMA   CA 94975

Pomegranate

Lunch hour, twenty-two floors up, 1925
The New York Times Photo Archives

BOX 808022   PETALUMA   CA 94975

Pomegranate

NEW YORK CITY
Photographs from **The New York Times**

Circus elephants parade on Fifth Avenue, 1921
The New York Times Photo Archives

BOX 808022   PETALUMA   CA 94975

Pomegranate

NEW YORK CITY
Photographs from **The New York Times**

Brooklyn Bridge, 1914
The New York Times Photo Archives

CA 94975

PETALUMA

BOX 808022

Pomegranate

NEW YORK CITY
Photographs from **The New York Times**

Times Square, crowd watching for World Series updates, 1920
The New York Times Photo Archives

BOX 808022   PETALUMA   CA 94975

Pomegranate

NEW YORK CITY
Photographs from **The New York Times**

Workers on TV tower of Empire State Building, 1950
The New York Times Photo Archives

BOX 808022   PETALUMA   CA 94975

Pomegranate

NEW YORK CITY
Photographs from **The New York Times**

Statue of Liberty centennial, July 4, 1986
Fred R. Conrad/The New York Times Photo Archives

BOX 808022   PETALUMA   CA 94975

Pomegranate

NEW YORK CITY
Photographs from The New York Times

City inspector checks a ride at Coney Island, 1959
Neal Boenzi/The New York Times Photo Archives

BOX 808022   PETALUMA   CA 94975

Pomegranate

NEW YORK CITY
Photographs from **The New York Times**

Officials activate Central Park sprinkler for the first time, 1928
The New York Times Photo Archives

BOX 808022   PETALUMA   CA 94975

Pomegranate

NEW YORK CITY
Photographs from **The New York Times**

Chrysler Building, 1930
The New York Times Photo Archives

BOX 808022   PETALUMA   CA 94975

Pomegranate

NEW YORK CITY
Photographs from **The New York Times**

Philippe Petit on tightrope at Cathedral of St. John the Divine, 1982
Fred R. Conrad/The New York Times Photo Archives

BOX 808022 PETALUMA CA 94975

Pomegranate

NEW YORK CITY
Photographs from **The New York Times**

View of Empire State Building from RCA Building, 1958
Robert Walker/The New York Times Photo Archives

CA 94975

PETALUMA

BOX 808022

Pomegranate

NEW YORK CITY
Photographs from 𝕮𝖍𝖊 𝕹𝖊𝖜 𝖄𝖔𝖗𝖐 𝕿𝖎𝖒𝖊𝖘

Lightning strikes Empire State Building, 1997
Chang W. Lee/The New York Times Photo Archives

BOX 808022   PETALUMA   CA 94975

Pomegranate

NEW YORK CITY
Photographs from **The New York Times**

Blizzard of confetti, Fifth Avenue, 1947
The New York Times Photo Archives

BOX 808022   PETALUMA   CA 94975

Pomegranate

NEW YORK CITY
Photographs from The New York Times

Times Square sleet storm, 1937
The New York Times Photo Archives

BOX 808022   PETALUMA   CA 94975

Pomegranate

NEW YORK CITY
Photographs from **The New York Times**

Winter's fury, 1914
International News Service/The New York Times Photo Archives

BOX 808022　PETALUMA　CA 94975

Pomegranate

NEW YORK CITY
Photographs from 𝕿𝖍𝖊 𝕹𝖊𝖜 𝖄𝖔𝖗𝖐 𝕿𝖎𝖒𝖊𝖘

The Woolworth Building from the Municipal Building, 1916
Edwin Levick/The New York Times Photo Archives

BOX 808022   PETALUMA   CA 94975

Pomegranate

New York City
Photographs from **The New York Times**

The *Akron* in flight over Manhattan, 1931
The New York Times Photo Archives

BOX 808022 PETALUMA CA 94975

Pomegranate

NEW YORK CITY
Photographs from **The New York Times**

Crowds at Stock Exchange on "Black Tuesday," 1929
The New York Times Photo Archives

BOX 808022   PETALUMA   CA 94975

Pomegranate

NEW YORK CITY
Photographs from **The New York Times**

V-J Day, Times Square, August 14, 1945
Patrick A. Burns/The New York Times Photo Archives

BOX 808022   PETALUMA   CA 94975

Pomegranate

NEW YORK CITY
Photographs from **The New York Times**

Manhattan skyline, 1962
Sam Falk/The New York Times Photo Archives

BOX 808022   PETALUMA   CA 94975

Pomegranate

NEW YORK CITY
Photographs from **The New York Times**

Third Avenue elevated train, c. 1952
Sam Falk/The New York Times Photo Archives

BOX 808022 PETALUMA CA 94975

Pomegranate

NEW YORK CITY
Photographs from **The New York Times**

Metropolitan Opera, 1938
The New York Times Photo Archives

BOX 808022   PETALUMA   CA 94975

Pomegranate

NEW YORK CITY
Photographs from **The New York Times**

St. Paul's Chapel and World Trade Center, 1975
Larry Morris/The New York Times Photo Archives

BOX 808022 PETALUMA CA 94975

Pomegranate

NEW YORK CITY
Photographs from **The New York Times**

Trading at the New York Stock Exchange, 1934
The New York Times Photo Archives

BOX 808022 PETALUMA CA 94975

Pomegranate

NEW YORK CITY
Photographs from **The New York Times**

The face of Liberty, 1982
Eddie Hausner/The New York Times Photo Archives

BOX 808022   PETALUMA   CA 94975

Pomegranate

NEW YORK CITY
Photographs from **The New York Times**

Autogiros over Manhattan, 1930
The New York Times Photo Archives

BOX 808022 PETALUMA CA 94975

Pomegranate

NEW YORK CITY
Photographs from **The New York Times**

Raising a flag at Ebbets Field, 1942
The New York Times Photo Archives

BOX 808022   PETALUMA   CA 94975

Pomegranate

NEW YORK CITY
Photographs from **The New York Times**

The Flatiron Building and Madison Square, c. 1910
The New York Times Photo Archives

BOX 808022   PETALUMA   CA 94975

Pomegranate